© 2021 Tom Huth

Published by
Sungold Editions
Santa Barbara

ISBN: 978-0-9991678-6-1

Holly's Last Adventure

documentary poems

by Tom Huth

Sungold Editions
2021

Contents

The Beach Shack	6
Zancudo	8
Nothing but Sand	10
The Boys from San Vito	12
Portent	14
Mr. Empathy	16
The Diagnosis	18
The Upside of Denial	20
Tiny Boxes	22
The Warm Breath of Italy	24

John of God	26
The Terrors of Withdrawal	28
One Step at a Time	30
A Spark of the Divine	32
No More to Prove	34
In the Moment	36
Pillow Talk	38
One Last Time	40
The Gravekeeper	42

The Beach Shack

We are walking the beach
in Belize in a warm rain
at the end of a good trip
when she fancies
    What if we had a place
    we could come back to
    whenever we wanted?
A beach house?
    Not a house exactly
A beach shack?
    Fruit trees in the yard
    mangoes papayas bananas
Porch railings
out of driftwood

The beach shack in paradise
my editors will love it
bougainvillea crawling
over the showerhead
like the expats
have in Yelapa

But we'd keep it simple
so we'd have less to lose
if the local situation
turned against us

Zancudo

Spanish for mosquito
a remote scattering
of unassuming cottages
on a wild Pacific beach
in a sweaty gulf called
the armpit of Costa Rica

    A few hundred natives
    a few dozen castaways
the teachers from Mendocino
gold miners from the Yukon
the woodworker from Aspen
the mailman from Quebec

My magazine makes it a series
The Eden Project they call it
Annie Leibovitz will shoot us
Then why the dark ruminations?

    My father died at 50
    I just turned 53
    Holly is 51
        Could this be
        our last big
        adventure?

Nothing but Sand

Chino Bob motorboats us
through mangrove channels
to the town of Golfito
a banana port gone bust

A lawyer helps us set up
a landholding corporation
named *La Palapa Pequena*
We ask feeble questions
about financial pitfalls
The lawyer grants
    There is always a risk
    but not a 90% risk
    It is only
We come forward in our chairs
            a normal risk

This contract is like Zancudo
built upon nothing but sand
Faith alone will be our guide
faith in the power of adventure
    over dim practicality
        over growing old itself

The Boys from San Vito

We bring aboard Agustin and Gerardo
brothers from a town whose menfolk
have always been workers of wood

Bang bang bang the shack is framed
Bang bang bang the tin roof up
    the beachfront deck
    the outdoor shower
    the winding steps
    to the bedroom
    in the treetops
Four hundred square feet
twenty thousand dollars
two months and change

Holly paints the outside a deep green
    and it sinks back into the jungle
        like it's been here all along

The boys from San Vito
announce *Hemos terminado*
They pack up their tools
    no speeches no hugs
by noon they are gone
the beach shack is ours

Portent

Our offices hammocks
hung between palm trees
carpets of pillowy sand
ceilings of layered fronds
driftwood stumps for tables
notebooks waiting to be filled

Holly writes children's books
about Rosita the tortilla lady
Santiago the vegetable vendor
Maria the fisherman's daughter
    who comes over to play

At sunrise while it's still cool
we run barefoot down the surfline
She swims laps while I ride waves
then the mangoes papayas bananas

Whatever made me think
    this could be
our last big adventure?

Doing yoga on the sand
our first winter here
stretching out her arms
in salute to the sun
my sweetheart notices
    that her fingers
        are trembling

Mr. Empathy

Back in Colorado next autumn
lying in bed watching football
her head tucked under my chin

Is she crying?
What's happening honey?
    Nothing
Elway dropping back to pass
Are you sure?
Flag on the play
    Something's wrong with me
Nothing's wrong with you
Did he fumble?
    Remember in Zancudo?
    those tremors?
Yeah?
Chiefs ball
    They're getting worse
Isn't it just what your mom had?
    It's more than that
I hug her tighter
Chiefs in Bronco territory
How do you know?
They settle for a field goal
She has nodded off
We can talk at halftime
but I can't feel anything
shaking inside

The Diagnosis

We thank the
neurologist

book our next
appointment

six months
from now

No urgency I guess
     Is that good?
Who knows?

We wait for
the elevator
in silence
two writers
so handy
with words

Got your purse?

She holds it out

I'm taking care
of her already

The Upside of Denial

I suggest we sit down
and face up to what
the future could bring
> *How would that help?*
> *I have hardly any symptoms*
> *Why talk about the future?*
Because it's unavoidable
> *But it's not here yet*

For 20 years Holly has devoted
two hours almost every morning
to Tibetan meditation and yoga
aspiring to live in the moment
Occasionally I mock her routines
if she does something unspiritual
like not loving me sufficiently
> Now I venture
You don't want to make a plan?

> *We'll work on things*
> *when they come up*
> *Whatever happens we'll*
> *have to deal with it*

If you have Parkinson's disease
> or even if you don't
maybe it's the best you can do
> live every day to the max
before destiny lowers the boom

Tiny Boxes

In sickness as in health
a free-range imagination

> It feels like a metal ball
> is rolling around inside me
>
> It feels like they've
> stuffed me with stucco
>
> It feels like I'm getting
> pulled over by a blizzard
>
> It feels like tiny boxes
> are holding me up
>
> It feels like my skin
> is being turned inside out
>
> It feels like my waist
> has gone down
>   one level
>
> It feels like
> my underpants
>   don't travel
>   at the same
>   speed

The Warm Breath of Italy

In the cliffside town of Vernazza
our room overlooks the Mediterranean
the belltower of a medieval church
the piazza with its ruined castle

At night we leave the windows open
to the sounds of merrymaking below
the mighty tolling of the bells
    You are in Italy they resound
as we nest in each other's arms

Three years out from the diagnosis
she can still hike a mile or two
on the paths of the Cinque Terre
If a train breaks down she can step
over the tracks to catch a new one
    I keep vigilant watch
Will this be her last time abroad?

In Calabria we slip into bed again
to merriment from the piazza below
    Between the sheets we feel
    the warm breath of Italy

The doctors didn't warn us about
this side-effect of her new drug
On 17 of our 18 nights in Italy
(I'm the official scorekeeper)
we succumb to love's tender call

*John
of
God*

    He lives in the jungle in Brazil
Has he dealt with Parkinson's?
    It isn't a body thing
Wouldn't you want a track record?
    It's a spiritual thing
Doesn't he operate with jackknives?
    You don't have to do that part
How can one guy cure everything?
    The kids could come visit
It isn't like we'd be living there
    I can see wearing white every day
Let's check another option
    It would eliminate my whole
    decision-making thing
What would?
    If everybody wore white
You can wear white around here
    It's not the same
Call me Tom of God

The Terrors of Withdrawal

It has happened every night
since she got off the meds
which turned her paranoid
and made her see things

    Tom!
What?
    Help me!
Help you what?
    Tom!
I'm right here
    Time!
Tom
    I'm dying!
Holly wake up

Can she even hear me?
I roll her onto her back
her eyes blank and spooky
possessed by some terror
neither awake nor asleep
but trapped in some
    inaccessible badland
        halfway between

Worse than the
disease itself
    every midnight
    for a year now

One Step at a Time

What a relief it would be
to sit down and hold hands
and treasure one another
and cry and cry and cry
> *Poor us poor us*
> *what happened*
> *to our lives?*
But dwelling on the big picture
would be admission of defeat
Our plight would seem unending

So we live
day by day
hour by hour
task by task
step by step
eat a meal
take a walk
let her nap
wake her up
do it again

keeping grief
locked inside
not realizing
that some day
the bill will
> come due

*A
Spark
of
the
Divine*

We stop seeing doctors
She confides to her healer
> I used to have more faith
> I'd read The Course in Miracles
> and I'd cry and I'd talk to God
> and I'd feel in touch with him

And now you're living it Holly
You're one of those people
you used to cry about

You already have within you
a spark of the divine
Demand of God that he show you
the path you should take

He doesn't need to cure you
to do any cheap parlor tricks
> Tell him
Show me how to get back to you
He cannot resist that prayer
He cannot refuse you

No More to Prove

Poking through the ruins
    of what-could-have-beens
        searching for positives

In her prime she used to fret
    there was never enough time
        to do all she wanted to do

Now she can relax
    Time is on her side
        There is no more to do

She doesn't have to prove herself
    by helping another child
        or writing another book

Doesn't have to be pretty
    doesn't have to be poised
        or perfect anymore

She is coming to settle
    in the embrace of an
        enduring serenity

In the Moment

Bedbound now
just 70 pounds
twenty years
under the spell

doesn't rage
against the dying
    of the light

doesn't bemoan her fate
She makes peace with it

or she cannot hear it
knocking at the door

She focuses only on what
is right in front of her
    a plate of fruit
    a familiar face
    a postcard from a son
The past has dropped away
The future has evaporated

She has arrived at the goal
of her spirit's expedition
her deepest adventure ever
living in the here and now

Pillow Talk

I kneel beside her bed
trying to understand what
she struggles to tell me
    her voice faint
    but insistent

Is she saying good-bye?
    I lean closer
her forehead warm against mine
Are these her final words?
Will I always have to wonder
    what she said?

I prompt
Whatever happens honey
I'll be okay
The kids will be okay

At last she summons the clarity
to pronounce in a froggy whisper
    We   need   more   butter

I lay a hand on her bony shoulder
I'll shop in the morning honey

She closes her eyes
    reassured

*One
Last
Time*

Awakened suddenly
middle of the night
the light coming on
over the stairway

footsteps ascending

already I know

Janet the caregiver
a consoling whisper
   She has passed

I walk downstairs
slip into her room
lie down beside her
cradled against her
one arm around her
soothing her still
sensing the warmth
sensing the person
sensing the Holly
departing her form
feeling her flesh
in my sorry hands
   one last time

The Gravekeeper

He drives up to our gold-rush cemetery
with a post-hole digger and an iron bar
    to bust open the earth
We carry the tools to Holly's site
    and mine as well some day
in an aspen grove I think she'll like

He plunges the bar into the stony soil
to loosen it from the fortress below
    We'll go down eighteen inches
    then we'll hit solid rock
    and that'll be it
burial a hard-earned privilege here

I take the post-hole digger
    lift out the loose dirt
        lean into her chamber
        smooth out the bottom

I tell the gravekeeper
I'll bring a shovel
to the memorial so her
sons can cover her ashes

The gravekeeper counsels
    Forget the shovel
    Let 'em fill it in
    with their hands

www.ingramcontent.com/pod-product-compliance
Lightning Source LLC
Chambersburg PA
CBHW010448010526
44118CB00021B/2538